We're born from the light,
fade to black,
and then …

the pure illumination
of spirit everlasting.

~ Candice James

Also by Paul Bluestein

Time Passages   (*Silver Bow Publishing 2020*)

Fade to Black

paul Bluestein

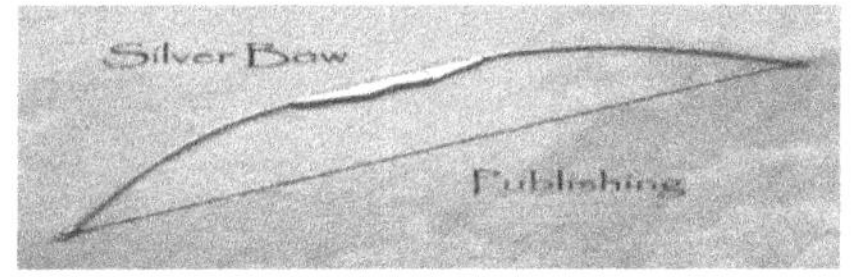

Silver Bow Publishing
720 Sixth Street, Box # 5
New Westminster, BC
CANADA   V3L3C5

Title: Fade to Black
Author: paul Bluestein
Cover Art: "Fade to Black" painting by Candice James
Cover Design: Candice James
Layout and Editing: Candice James
ISBN: 9781774031858(print)
ISBN: 9781774031865 (e-book)
© 2021 Silver Bow Publishing

Library and Archives Canada Cataloguing in Publication

Title: Fade to black / Paul Bluestein.
Names: Bluestein, Paul, 1947- author.
Identifiers: Canadiana (print) 20210299150 | Canadiana (ebook) 20210299169 | ISBN 9781774031858
   (softcover) | ISBN 9781774031865 (HTML)
Subjects: LCGFT: Poetry.
Classification: LCC PS3602.L82 F33 2021 | DDC 813/.6—dc23
info@silverbowpublishing.com
Website: www.silverbowpublishing.com

To my wife, Lynda,
who has always brought out the best in me,
even when it was hard to find.

Table of Contents

Awakening

Jazz Trio

Guitar

> Fingers,
> glide gracefully
>   string to string,
> fret to fret.
> Each note a drop of rain
> from clouds of jazz.

Piano

> Two hands   skitter across
> the black and white keyboard.
> Spiders spinning silken threads of
> smooth jazz.

Drums

> Cymbals, high-hat
> snare and tom-toms.
> A bebop, hot funk
> Afro-Cuban heartbeat.
> Rhythms like twelve-year old Scotch
> shot straight to the soul.
> Cool...

Subway Benediction

Running for the subway shuttle
from Grand Central to Broadway,
I heard music drifting through
an open door.

I swung into the car and there he was.
Long-haired, bearded; standing in the aisle
with his mismatched socks on display,
singing '*Somewhere Over the Rainbow*'
in a voice so open and sunlit
that I forgot I was underground.

Even the wheels squealing
as the train rocked along the tracks
could not pull me out of the song
spinning through the crowded car
like a spider's web, holding us fast.

A hat on the floor in front of him
held some silver and paper
and I added my thanks.

As I left the train and headed for the exit,
I could still hear him singing
to the empty car, words that poured
out into the station and were reflected
by white-tile walls, spattering
us all with red, violet and green.

In Praise of Horn Players

Inspired by "So What" by Miles Davis

You can hear the sound of horn players
in wedding-cake concert halls,
cramped jazz clubs from LA to Harlem
and second line funerals in New Orleans.

They have wakened soldiers from their sleep
at daybreak, called them to battle in noonday sun
and laid them to final rest in evening shadows.
Dizzy playing bebop brought fans to their feet
but Miles is sittin' down bourbon and blues.

There's nothing like it in nature.
It's a human sound.
Cries of joy, sadness and anger
over thousands of years.

The great horn players speak
The Mother of All Languages
with an eloquence older than words

Amanuensis

The footprints of semiquavers and minims
leap up and down the staircase
that is the lines and spaces of the staff.

Accidentals, scattered amongst
          Every Good Boy Doing Fine
                    and
          All Cows that Eat Grass,
wait in the expectant silence
before the music begins,
to trip us on the journey from
whole tone to whole tone

With ornamentals and articulations,
I can transcribe precisely
the composer's what and how,
but not the passion or imagination.

Look beyond the bars of the staves
that make prisoners of the players.

Ignore the distracting precision
that notes and rhythm demand.

Discover the musician's hidden path
          not from brain to paper,
          but from heart to fingers
          and out into the world.

One of the Wind Chime Clan

The wind chimes hang lifeless
on the tree branches like poets or prophets
finally silenced.
Rigid, hollow bodies unmoving
in the summer stillness.

But calling them lifeless is a lie.

They are no deader than a trumpet
asleep in its case until it's kissed awake.
They're simply waiting for the wind.

Or maybe they're introverts,
and need to be encouraged
to join the conversation.

I understand wind chimes' lives.
Once, I was one of them.

Then you arrived
like an autumn storm
and reminded me how to sing.

Snowy Egret

Unmoving as a palace guard,
only the afternoon wind
ruffling the feathers of its crown
and a blinking eye
betray the egret's statue ruse.

Braced on golden slippers
against the swirling current,
poised to strike, it bides its time,
unmindful of the osprey circling overhead
or the cat that roams the shoreline.

Waiting for a destined fish
to keep its appointment with Samsara,
this egret knows nothing of philosophers or saints,
but it does understand the geometry of tides
and the symmetry of survival.

I could learn the secrets
of patience and silent devotion.
sitting beside a pond in spring.

Exodus II

I climbed up
to shout you from the rooftop.
Fingernails and scrabbling feet,
searching for a place to stand,
immersed in the visions flowing from
your daydreams and nightmares.

But before I could speak
the desert heat baked your words,
leaving them flat and tasteless.
Bread with no meaning to make it rise.

Alone, watched only
by the blind eye of the sun,
I told myself "Climb down".
Too late,
I felt my feet
slipping on mossy, rotting shakes
and could not keep from falling
like a penny in a wishing well,
to hard truth and broken bones below.

Mother-father-brother-sister
teacher - stranger.
It's me,
wandering in the wilderness you made.

Heretic

"Well, I'll be damned!"
and they all agreed.
My life was not to their liking.
More like striking a match
in a tinder-dry field;
a weapon to wield in defiance.

Seeking neither latitude of wrong
nor longitude of right, I turned
from their lamps and their light,
and finding no prayer to pray
I walked slowly away
into the deepening night.

Prophets

The prophets, still as statues,
stand listening for the sound of Gabriel's horn.
Ravens, flying on the wind,
like restless souls who've sinned,
race on before the storm.

On wings of night,
they rise to flee cathedral bells
that tell of secrets past
and warn of judgments yet to be,
while I wait patiently for angels to whisper
they are watching over me.

Sometimes Crazy Is All There Is

From the corner of my eye,
I noticed a spider leave its web,
spun between a picture frame and the wall.

As it finger-walked
across the wide polished plain of my desk,
I picked up a notebook,
intending to crush the spindly trespasser.

Then, as the paperback bomb
was ready to fall,
I hesitated, reconsidered,
and let the spider continue on.

I declared a day of amnesty,
a 24-hour no-die zone.

I know it sounds crazy
to think this will change anything,
but ... sometimes crazy is all there is.

Yes, I know ...

Mommy, look! The dinosaur is in its cave under the couch
* * *

Mama, today Ms. Jackson said that California
used to be part of Mexico. Texas too!
* * *

Mother, I just can't wear this to school.
Nobody wears this. It's so lame.
* * *

M-o-o-o-o-m, stop yelling at me to clean up my room!
It's MY room and I like it that way!
* * *

Wow Mom! You bought me tickets
to the Green Day concert!!! You said I couldn't go.
* * *

Ma, graduation day is June 3rd. Dad asked if he could come.
* * *

How are you Mom? You were right.
College isn't as easy as I thought it would be.
* * *

Mother, Sean and I are thinking about moving in together.
* * *

Mama, if it's OK with you,
I'd like Dad to walk me down the aisle.
* * *

I'm sorry I haven't called in a while,
but you know how it is. Work and all.
* * *

Thanks for letting me know about Dad.
Even after the two of you got divorced, he and I, well ...
you know
* * *

Christ, Mother. If I knew pregnancy would be this hard,
I would have ... never mind. It'll be fine.
* * *

Grammy, Look! The dinosaur is in its cave under the couch
* * *

Nothing's Lost

Her hands hold the guitar tentatively,
like a new mother,
while her fingers struggle
with half-remembered folk-songs,
first learned 50 years ago,
during her sexual revolution;
during her war for independence.

These are hands that moved on from chords
to carrying signs at sit-ins,
wore a wedding ring,
wrote a thesis,
raised children and a husband.

Hands that tried to hold tight to a life
that was snatched away while she was busy
helping with homework
and making ends meet
when there was more month
at the end of the money.

Now, as she picks at the strings,
the guitar begins to sing again,
to find its long-stilled voice;
and, slowly, it all comes back to her.

Black Walnut

Modesty fits you
           like a badly made dress,
                  loose and shapeless
           hiding the person underneath.

You don't have to
                bend down, or lie down
                     for anybody.

                    It's an insult
                 to the god who made you a tree
            to go around tangled and tight
                 like a barberry bush.
Stand up
tall and
strong,
dangerous
as a black
walnut.
Stretch out
your arms
to hold
up the sky
and feel
the core
of the
world
beneath
your feet.
            Live in the sunlight
           and if anyone tries
                 to throw shade at you,
                     stick a branch in his eye
               and call it just.

Taking your place in the world is no sin.

Goodbye

I can hear you gently talking
but I can't hear what you say.
I think you want to tell me you're leaving
even while you want to stay.

I can hear your voice beside me;
your words are shining in your eyes.
I wish I could make it easy;
always has been hard to say goodbye.

I know there's things you must be learning;
growing older questions who and why:
I hope you'll find all your answers.
I hope the growing light won't hurt your eyes.

Just stay with me until the morning;
then you can leave me behind.
Close your eyes, just go to sleep;
try to rest it easy on your mind.

Sunlight & Shadow

Curios

The shelves of the curio cabinet
display the truths and lies of a life.
Pictures of distant places
and distant children stand side by side
with baby shoes and wedding invitations.
A tarnished medal and faded purple ribbon;
memorials to wounds that will not heal.

But beneath the shelves
are key-locked drawers
that hold mysteries and secrets
too fragile to be exposed to a judging sun.
Keepsakes strung on strands of memory
like dimly winking Christmas lights.
Ornaments for late-night hours, sitting quietly,
lost to the world around me,
haunted by thoughts of things
that might have been.

December Morning:
Second-stage Sleep

Morning light, that thief of sleep,
creeps slowly into the room
through a cracked window
and blue-black cold slithers
under the crooked door.

Wrapped warm in a Pumpkin-Seed quilt,
I have no intention of surrendering sleep
though the bedside clock tries to prod me
into wakefulness with its insistent buzz
until I slap it into silence,
like I would an annoying mosquito.

Listening to the muffled
chorus of wind chimes,
accompanied by shards of ice
and a hurricane of snow
ticking against the windows,
I drift back out on the current of dreams,
away from the long New England winter.

Hard Lessons of Winter

The wrens living in the red barn birdhouse
moved south at the end of summer,
leaving me to clean up after them;
but it's just like wrens to be so inconsiderate.

When I had finished, the house looked inviting
and though it was visited from time to time
it remained empty
until an October frost had whitewashed its walls
and polished the roof with ice.

Then a black-capped chickadee arrived,
crossed the threshold and emerged
with a chirping claim to her new home.
From safely distant perches,
grackles, juncos and a wary cardinal eyed the newcomer,
twittering "Who invited you, who invited you?"

November was beset with tree-branch drama
about territory and pecking order
accompanied by anxious hopping, fluttering of wings
and curiosity among the onlookers.

But when the wind and snow of December arrived,
bringing the need to simply survive,
they put aside arguments and misunderstandings,
sheltered in their winter homes,
and dreamed of spring.

New Year

Fifteen minutes to midnight.
December thirty-first.
On the table beside my chair,
a battered wooden box holds
twelve months of disappointments
and regrets saved up for this night.
The letter written to my mother, still unsent.
The pink slip from Mr. Jameson.
"Thank you for your submission" rejections and
"Insufficient Funds" notices.

As the ball in Times Square
slides toward a new year,
I lay these sad paper corpses,
one by one, in a chipped bowl,
strike a match and watch them burn,
then gather the ashes in my palms,
wringing my hands until the skin
is gritty and stained by memories
that cut like broken glass.

With Auld Lang Syne ringing in my ears,
I stand scrubbing my hands,
trying to wash off the past
and begin the new year
as fresh and clean as the snow
falling outside my window.

January Daybreak

The mist is rising from the earth
like steam from my cup of coffee.
Blue jays and black-capped chickadees
silently share their perch
with a Revlon-red cardinal.

Ice tears along the branches of the trees
flare in the sunrise,
looking like tiny Christmas lights
that have hidden in the forest,
escaping an eleven month sentence
of solitary confinement in a dark attic.

The only sounds
are the ticking of the kitchen clock
and the occasional creak
or clank of an aging house.

Soon there will be traffic,
the morning news
and snow shovels scraping streets,
but right now, there is quiet
and time to wonder,
to watch the dogs sleeping in a curl
and wish the clock would stop
for just a little while.

Wild Onions

Spring came and,
as they always do,
the wild onions
poked their miserable shoelace shoots
up out of the ground.

Like rude subway riders,
they crowd in close
to young, delicate flowers,
trying to push them aside
as if they owned the ground
in which they grew.

They may not think of themselves as weeds,
but that is what they are.
Oh, some people would say
wild onions are vegetables,
like parsnips or beets,
but I say they are weeds
and they will find no comfort in *my* garden.

I will unsheathe my spade and stainless steel claw
and do battle with the April invaders;
root them out wherever I find them
and let them serve as a lesson to mint
that might be thinking of becoming
delinquent, wild and uncontrollable.

Stone Bench at Noon

Cloistered at noon in a Zen Garden I sat
cross-legged on the centered stone bench
while a fence-sitting squirrel,
on the lookout for danger, stood watch.

The sounds of the Southern-Pacific
in the distance and an airliner
descending along its flight path,
swirled tranquility and quiet contemplation
together with 21st century chaos;
but I was glad just to be in that place,
shaded by the tulip trees.

Tell Me About Blue

'Tell me about blue', he said.
'The color of the sea
and the sky is a mystery,
as meaningless to me as
my darkness is to you'.

'In winter,' I replied, 'blue is the feeling
in your face and hands as a nor'easter howls
through the steel and glass canyons of the city.'

Winter blue is the sound of "Stormy Monday"
or Dylan growling out "Everything Is Broken".
But in spring, blue can be Irving Berlin's "Blue Skies",
as light and airy as the sound of sheets hanging
on the line, snapping in a lilac April breeze.

Blue is the taste of blueberry ice cream on a warm day
when the yellow of the sun and the blue of the sky
mix together to make the green month of May
and you can hear whispered promises of summer
in the rustling of the leaves.

Summer in Black & White

Asphalt parking lots,
carved by forward-slash lines,
unfurl from ribbon-roads
softening in the summer heat.

White-washed buildings stand rooted,
painting black shadows on pale concrete steps,
while black & white police cars drift by.

The morning paper arrives with news
struggling to find daylight in our darkness.

Why is it that we ignore living
under a blue sky and yellow sun,
amidst Jackson Pollack flower fields,
and choose, instead, to circle one another
in uncompromising orbits, like stars
separated by vast black swaths of night?

Last Day of Summer

The calendar on my desk insists
summer's visit is over, but I'm not ready
to say my goodbyes just yet,
as I hear a shout of "Marco",
answered by a laughing "Polo",
the neighbor children playing in the pool.

The Good Humor ice cream truck
is coming around the corner
and I haven't yet put away my khakis or T-shirts.

Sparrows are singing like it's June,
the clouds are as white as Tide-washed sheets
hanging on the line, drying in a hot July breeze
and the cicadas are whirring in the grass,
as if this was still August.

If I just act like summer
isn't packed up
and ready to leave,
maybe I can fool autumn
into thinking it arrived early
and keep it waiting outside the door
until I'm ready to let it in.

Leaf Fall

The leaf fall of autumn is prelude
to the snowfall of winter.

While wind rattles their branches,
birches and maples
toss red and copper confetti
into October air,
like bright pennies
thrown into a wishing well,
spinning down
without a sound.

They gather
in drifts that children-at- heart
will wade through just to sink
knee-deep into the smell
and hear the crunch,
like breaking the ice frosting mounds
of December snow.

But snow drifts and prism leaves,
too soon, turn from wondrous
to roadside heaps of dirty brown,
swept aside by unrelenting time.

Dusk

Shady Grove, USA

There are no groves in Shady Grove.
In fact, there is no shade.
Just concrete and Costco
and condos and Wendy's
and RVs and Walgreens.

There is no view of the harbor on Harborview,
no lanterns on Lantern Road
and not a tree remains on Chestnut Street.
Even the light from the streetlamps
looks tired and bruised
while pretty place-names are thrown
like drop-cloths meant to cover up
the broken windows, broken promises
and broken spirits of small town America

Snowy Dove

No need to take any notice.
I'm just passing through; you're just passing by.
Walking your easy streets,
one wrong turn from *my* hard road.
I am just some broken cement or
an icy patch in winter. Walk around me
like you'd avoid a fallen log,
lest I become kindling
to stoke the fires of your worried dreams.

I will wrap myself in the shreds of my dignity
while you pull your coat tighter
to hide your helpless heart.

I will become a snowy dove
perched in a white-blossoming dogwood.
Bird invisible.

Three Days of Hope

In the gray morning,
a ragged line forms outside the door.
People wait while rain
runs off their shoulders and shoes.

Inside, volunteers count cans of tuna
and loaves of bread.
There are bags of rice,
peanut butter and jars of jam –
food and hope, doled out in three-day parcels –
the best we can do even while we know
it's not enough.
Still, we listen to funny/sad stories,
ask about children or parents,
and carry bags to cars
that are sometimes also homes.

When, finally, we have nothing left to give,
we close the door and,
surrounded by empty shelves,
realize again how close we are
to asking if we can please have
one more box of cereal.

View from the 23rd Floor

From the perch of my apartment,
23 floors above the crowded street,
cigar-shaped chimney swifts
swoop and dart against the setting sun.
A "V" of geese races the clouds
of an approaching storm;
A murmuration of starlings swims
through the sky, flashing and wheeling
like a school of fish in perfect synchrony.

Not at all like the pods of people
washed up on the concrete shore below.

With paddling arms, graceless legs
and clumsy tortoise-shell backpacks,
they crawl toward home,
pushing and bumping
through the late afternoon sea,
unmindful of the show
just above their heads,
but far beyond their reach.

What to Do with the Bee?

Drifting on a raft in the pool, trying to forget
my 24 on-call that ended at 7 AM,
the water rocks me gently,
lapping away the accumulated
adrenaline of the long shift.

While I watch fish-scale clouds
in the morning sky,
a bee lands nearby
like a fat, black and yellow drop of rain,
buzzing and spinning,
trying to escape the watery trap.

What do I do with the bee?
Leave its fate to chance or the god of bees?
Hit it with a flip-flop and provide the mercy
of a sudden and painless death?
Or scoop it up with my hand -
a suburban deus ex machina -
and toss it back into the land of the living?

If I do that, I might get stung.
Should I risk that to save a bee's life?

What if it was a man, who, in his panic,
might drown me even while he saves himself?
Who lives? Who dies?
And who decides?

I don't know, and I don't want to know.
But in 22 hours, I'll put my MD back on
and walk into an ICU
where questions do have to be answered..

Ungewunscht

The dusty synagogue window looked out
onto the narrow Austrian street below.
Unterbergstrasse; where it began.
What the world called Kristallnacht,
and Jews called the beginning of the end.

The photograph on the wall,
behind a battered frame and glass
cracked and dirty like the window,
was of that same street in November 1938.
Chained at both ends,
crowded with people
beneath a banner that stretched
from one side of the street to the other,
from one side of Europe to the other.
A banner that read "Juden Ungewunscht,"
Jews unwelcome.

On the walls of the house, I read
the inscribed names of the dead,
and, looking again at the photograph,
wondered if I was seeing the past,
or perhaps some lurking tomorrow.

Through the Perilous Fight

* * * * * * from the corner of my eye, what I mistook
 * * * * *   to be a falling leaf was instead
* * * * * * a falling bird, hurtling toward the treetops,
clutching at the last shreds of cloud, blinded by
the sun, shrieking at the crowd below.
Wind tearing at bloodied blue and white-starred feathers
leaving useless broken wings.
I did not see the tattered body crater into open hands,
hoping to save it from the dust
but I did hear the footsteps of chaos coming

A Taste for the Game

The green baize on the table
looks inviting as a freshly washed and ironed sheet.

Cubes of blue chalk sit like spectators on the rails
while the rainbow rack of balls,
solids and stripes in Crayola colors,
wait for the kiss of the cue ball and the snick
of the counters on the wire overhead.

Pool is geometry and physics,
muscle-memory and nerve,
cigarette smoke and Scotch
stirred by the players into a jittering stew
peppered with swagger and money.

No one warns you that a taste for the game
can obscure the danger lurking in the pockets –
black holes that can swallow up a life.

Side of the Road

Get out there on the road
and you'll see
broken, battered dreams
and disappointments discarded
in the breakdown lane.

Not like squirrels or deer,
killed by four-wheel predators.

Their story is no mystery.

But what about the stuffed plush tiger
that should be asleep on a child's bed,
not dying in the shadow of a guardrail?

     A woo
     den chai
     r in piec
     es,
lying in the left-lane weeds.

A black lace bra.

Wreckage that calls out "why"?
but we don't hear a sound
as we hurry past.

Quiet Voice

Traffic stalls, the office calls;
the weekend's come and gone.
There was a road you traveled,
but it's not the one you're on.
You're looking for a turn-out
or perhaps an exit sign;
just a place where you can stop
and listen for that quiet voice inside.

Seasons change.
You rearrange the pictures on the wall.
You're going here, going there,
going nowhere real at all.
You need some time to just be still
after everything's been tried.
Just a place where you can stop
and listen for that quiet voice inside.

Life is rushing by so fast
you can't see what's ahead or past.
You just run on and hope to last
and somehow find the time
to listen for that quiet voice inside.

Night

Ghosts

The dogs stand riveted at the door,
separated from the night
by the thin veil of a screen.

The streets (to my eyes) are silent
and empty -
not even a moth,
fluttering in the washed-out yellow
of the flickering streetlamp.

But the dogs see … something.
Ears pricked, eyes fixed,
still as statues, they watch.

"A falling leaf", you say.
"Some night bird in the branches", you say.

Or is it the parade of the unseen passing?

When I have left this world,
will my companions see me in a shadow
or hear me in the wind?

Beyond the Clouds

If I could see beyond the clouds
what would *there* be?
As I stand *here*
(attached by the gravity of my life
to this two foot parcel of earth)
nothing *there* seems clear.

Will *there* be an endless green sea
on which I might float (or walk)?
But neither my eyes nor mind
reach enough,
so I am like a shell
washed up on some beach.
stretching toward forever in every direction.

One day the sky may clear
and I may understand
the mystery I am living.
I will *be* beyond the clouds,
inside a limitless blue box.
Sky end to end, side to side.

Until then?
The ink of my thoughts
will drop from the clouds like rain
and bloom upon a page.

I'll watch butterflies
light on leaves like orange flames.
and know that it is enough for now.

A Suit for My Father

Michail fled to a new country
with nothing but a bag of clothes
and a few kopecs in his pocket.
But he made his way in America
and began a family that would honor
and remember him after he died,
the year I was twelve.

Sam the Tailor on South Street
made me a suit for the funeral.
My first suit. My first funeral.
It made me feel like
standing in a winter rain,
wet tears for Micha, my father
and frozen by fear of a grown-up world.

In the years that have passed,
there have been many suits,
many friends and family lost
and although I've outgrown the fear,
I have yet to dry the tears
or forget the feeling of my first suit;
a suit for my father.

Hilltop Cemetery

Come midday, we set off for Hilltop,
the Shannon family cemetery
in Middle of Nowhere, South Texas,
near Tilden.

T, whose given name was Louis
but everyone called by his middle initial,
sat in the front seat between his children.
Cousin Pat followed in the Chevy S-10.
The bed of the pick-up,
most often loaded with feed or fencing
or blowtorches for burning pear,
today carried only shovels.

Walking to the place where
earlier in the day a hole had been dug,
we could read names and dates
on graves of generations past.
Children who died from diphtheria,
women who died in childbirth
or from the Spanish flu.
Men who died in war.

T's son placed his father's ashes in the ground
and we stood holding hands in the caliche dust and heat,
spoke remembrances and recited prayers.

Afterward, we took up the shovels,
mended the wounded earth and said goodbye,
having sent T home.
No preacher, no choir.
Just relatives, some friends
and the live oaks to watch over him.

Newton's First Law

A body in motion stays in motion
unless acted upon by an unbalanced force.

There are times I may appear to be at rest,
but I am, truthfully, in constant motion.
My chest rises and falls with each breath
and I feel heartbeats driving blood
to the far corners of me.

The atoms of my brain sing as they spin,
the perfect fifths of angels
and the tritones of the devil.
Harmony and dissonance,
side by side, decade after decade.

Someday, I will be dragged to a stop
        by the friction of time ...
            but until then,
I'll celebrate the unrelenting momentum of life
        before that sly unbalanced force
            comes creeping like a thief.

Short Walk at Sunset

The old man and his old dog walk slowly,
their autumn shadows stretched out long
ahead of them.

Behind them, the sun fights to remain in the sky
even though it has lost this contest
for billions of years and will soon,
in a green flash, surrender to the night ,
only to rise up again in the morning,
            born again.

For the old man, it is a short walk
at the end of a long day
and he will, like the sun,
be on the other side of the world,
out of sight and in darkness.

For now though, there will be shared food,
the evening news, and time to rest
in the chair by the window
while he watches his old dog's flank
rise and fall with each breath.

Pale and No Wings to Fly

Lying in the grass,
beside the rose bush I was dead-heading,
the world has turned upside-down.

A trapeze-artist circus squirrel
is performing at the top of the leafy green tent
for an audience of indifferent starlings;
and wind chimes, hanging beneath the pergola,
call to me like distant church bells.
I consider how strange the descending half-orange
overhead would look if it was a lime,
as the cut-grass smell of summer
takes me back to Tennessee,
lying in a field, watching cat-clouds
stalk across the sky.

A crow, sitting unmoved on a nearby limb
seems to stare down at me with disdain
for being so pale and having no wings to fly
while the tree watches the scene
with its single knot-hole eye
beneath an arched woody brow.

I feel like I could rest here
forever in the fading light
and I want to tell my wife,
kneeling beside me,
but the lowering sky pressing
down on my chest has left me breathless.

Besides, I'm not sure she would hear me
over the wail of the approaching sirens.

I Used to Wish

I hear it before I can see it,
like the sound of distant thunder.
Then, the cloud-curtain opens
and there is a jetliner glinting in the sunlight,
painting white contrails like railroad tracks
on a flat blue canvas of sky.

The passengers can't see me
staring up, wondering who they are
and where they are bound
but nonetheless knowing that sorrows
and celebrations, triumph and tragedy
are packed together for a few hours,
sitting side by side.

I used to wish I was traveling with them,
on some adventure of my own.
But not anymore.

Post-It

The cheat- sheet
in the palm of my eighth-grade hand
reminding me
that the Battle of Hastings was fought in 1066
has been replaced sixty-six years later
by a Post-It note on the bathroom mirror
that simply reads

Take your pills
There's cinnamon toast
and coffee in the kitchen.
I Love You

She puts it there every morning
to remind me the battle isn't over yet.

Acknowledgements

The following poems first appeared in:

"Jazz Trio"
Muddy River Poetry Review, 2019
"Subway Benediction"
The Big Windows Review
[Online May 11/Issue 24, August]
"Amanuensis"
Wellington Street Review
"One of the Wind Chime Clan"
Waymark Literary Magazine, 2020
"Snowy Egret"
Aji Magazine, 2020
"Exodus II"
House Press, December 2019
"Heretic"
Penumbra 2019
"Prophets"
The Broken Plate, 2019
"Sometimes Crazy Is All There Is"
Loch Raven Review, 2021
"Nothing's Lost"
Welter Online, 2020
"Black Walnut"
The Long River Review, 2021
"Hard Lessons of Winter"
Dwelling Literary, 2021
"New Year"
Sandy River Review, 2021
"January Daybreak"
Nixes Mate Magazine, 2021
"Wild Onions"
North of Oxford, 2021

"Stone Bench at Noon"
	Minnow Literary Magazine, 2021
"Tell Me About Blue"
	Skylight 47, 2021
"Shady Grove"
	River & South, 2020
"Snowy Dove"
	Apricity Magazine, 2020
"Three Days of Hope"
	El Portal, 2020
"View From the 23rd Floor"
	Juniper 2021
"What to Do with the Bee"
	Schuylkill Valley Journal, 2020
"Ungewunscht"
	River & South, 2020
"Ghosts"
	Verse-Virtual, 2019
"Beyond the Clouds"
	The Foxglove Journal, 2018
"A Suit for My Father"
	Pure Slush, 2021
"Hilltop Cemetery"
	Loch Raven Review, 2021
"Newton's First Law"
	The Phoenix, 2021
"Short Walk at Sunset"
	Bookends Review, 2021
"Pale & No Wings to Fly"
	Willawaw Journal 2021
"I Used to Wish"
	*Scribes*Micro*Fiction, 2021*
	Inaugural Issue

Author Profile

65

paul Bluestein is a physician (done practicing) and a blues guitar player (still practicing). He grew up in Philadelphia, and currently lives in Connecticut with Lynda,his wife, and a flat-coated retriever named Tucker.

paul's book, "Time Passages", won 1st Prize in the Book of Poetry Category at the 2020 Connecticut Press Club Awards

www.ingramcontent.com/pod-product-compliance
Lightning Source LLC
Chambersburg PA
CBHW071357200726
48294CB00004B/1202